SURVIVING
YOUR FRIEND'S
DIVORCE

SURVIVING YOUR FRIEND'S DIVORCE

10 Rules to Help You Both

Mary Kay Leatherman

ACTA Publications
Chicago, Illinois

Surviving Your Friend's Divorce
10 Rules to Help You Both
by Mary Kay Leatherman

Edited by Gregory F. Augustine Pierce
Cover Design by Tom A. Wright
Typesetting by Garrison Publications

Special thanks to Sr. Barbara Markey, Sr. Marie Micheletto, Michael Wave Leatherman, and the Family Life Office of the Archdiocese of Omaha for their support and help in preparing this book.

Copyright © 1996 by Mary Kay Leatherman

Published by: ACTA Publications
Assisting Christians To Act
4848 N. Clark Street
Chicago, IL 60640
312-271-1030

Library of Congress Catalog number: 95-083427

ISBN: 0-87946-135-7

Printed in the United States of America

00 99 98 97 96 5 4 3 2 1 First Edition

CONTENTS

DEDICATION

To all my
friends and relatives
who survived
my divorce,
especially
my mother
and father.

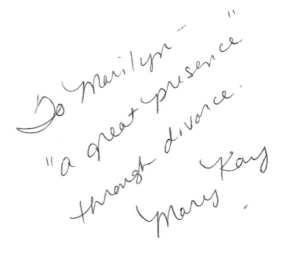

Introduction

Memories of the year immediately following my divorce are blurry. I do remember one incident very clearly, though. The doorbell rang on one of the usual chaotic days at my house. The man standing at the door in a dark suit and sporting a very bad haircut held a shabby briefcase in one hand and a tiny card in the other. Over the din of my barking dog and chattering toddler, he persisted with his pitch:

"Are you aware of the troubles in the world today?"

I refrained from the sarcastic response that came to my mind, smiled politely, and pushed the dog back from the door.

"Is God missing from your life?" he repeated. "Have you not let him in?"

I smiled again at his presumptuous arrogance, but I let him continue.

"May I suggest that you spend more time reacquainting yourself with the Lord. Many people today are actually very unaware of the truths hidden in the Bible, since they busy themselves with unnecessary obstacles."

I looked at my watch, since I had less than a half hour to get my sick child to a doctor's appointment. But the man would not take the hint.

"People have turned away from the Lord. My wife and I are constantly amazed at the violence, the homelessness, the high rate of divorce."

Bingo. He had said the magic buzz word: divorce. He had my attention, however momentarily.

"It surprises me how quickly couples give up on their marriages," he said, noticing my reaction. "In this throwaway world, most people take the easy way out...."

I didn't hear much more, because I was too angry and hurt. How should I reply to Mr. Holy-Man-Knocking-on-My-Door? I considered asking him if he knew what it was like for a person of faith to fail at marriage, but I knew that he did not. I also knew that I did know, because I was one.

I quickly imagined many questions I would like to ask him. Was he aware that most divorced people are not particularly happy about being divorced? Did he realize that many people leave a marriage in fear for their very life? Did he know that many people have no choice in their divorce?

I wanted to tell him, "The situation is not so cut and dried, Mr. Self-Righteous-with-the-Bad-Haircut-and-Shabby-Briefcase. It surprises me daily how many Christians like you do not understand the situation of those who bear the burden of divorce. If you really wanted to help me, you'd never take the approach you have."

Instead, I quietly responded, "Yes, the world does have many problems today. I am, however, very happy with my faith and religion, so I'll just take your card. Thank you."

It was that man's lucky day. I shut the door instead of ordering my dog to attack him.

□□□

My visitor, with his good intentions but terrible approach, probably had a genuine desire to help me. His lack of understanding and compassion, however, left me with my pain intact and possibly even a little deeper.

Was he a stereotype? A caricature of those who try to help others?

Well, yes and no. Most people do not go door to door trying to make other people feel badly about themselves. But they do find themselves in situations all the time where they are called upon to be supportive of others without having the slightest idea what the right thing to do or say might be.

The anger and frustration I felt that day were caused more by my need for real help in coming to terms with my divorce than this man's clumsy attempts to "save my soul." I knew that I needed to find a way to deal with what I thought should have been the headline of each day's news: Mary Kay was divorced! But I needed real help, not judgment or easy advice.

□□□

I turned first to books. I looked through the shelves of the library for a glimpse of hope. In the months following my husband's flight from our home, I read everything I could get my hands on that might help fill the continuous sick feeling I had in the pit of my stomach. I felt helpless, with a six month old baby and a deflated self-image. Yet I knew that I had to survive—for my child, for myself, for my other loved ones. I read everything, looking for one golden answer that might jump from one of the pages.

Of course, it never did. Oh, the books helped. They gave me practical advice and a sense that others had survived the experience of divorce. But after a while, I began to realize that much more important than what I learned from these books were the support, encouragement and love I received from my relatives, friends, co-workers and counselor. The "golden answers"—and there were many—that I sought eventually came, more often than not, from them as they patiently listened and encouraged me to reclaim my self-esteem and self-respect.

Despite their help, however, I recognized that often those supporting me seemed pained themselves. Their faces were often twisted with sadness and frustration. It seemed that they, too, were not sure what to do. "I don't understand you anymore," they would say. Or, "I'm not sure what to say."

□□□

Several years later, after I have successfully overcome my divorce, even to the point of marrying a wonderful second husband, I remember the frustration of my family and friends in helping me to deal with my divorce. I realize that, like myself, they were unsure of how to react, what to do, how to help. I also began to understand that they, too, had survived my divorce. They, too, had had to deal with the breakup of my first marriage and with their own emotions, losses and changes.

Helping them had not even been on my radar screen at the time. I was struggling to survive myself. I had neither the time nor the energy to worry about them!

Now I do. As I return to those library shelves on divorce, I now see that there is a book missing, a very important book. It is a book for those who are trying to survive the divorce of a friend or a relative themselves while at the same time being of real help to the person going through the divorce.

I realize now that my friends and relatives had valid questions about their role in my divorce that I could not answer at the time because I did not know the answers myself. They may not have recognized it, but even through the fog of my tears and self-doubt I could see their anguish and sense their frustration. A combination of their own loss of a friend or relative (my departed spouse) and a justified fear of not choosing just the right words of advice or consolation for me created a noticeable reticence on their part, which I often took for lack of interest or support.

It is for them that I have written this book, both as a belated "thank you" for the help that they did give and as a resource for them and others (myself included) who will most certainly be faced more than once with the task of surviving the divorce of a friend or relative.

□□□

I have written the book in the form of ten "rules" that I think must be followed if you are to be successful. These "rules" are merely tools to help you accept the proper role for yourself in the divorce of your friend or relative and to avoid some pitfalls along the way. You will find that several accounts are included from my own personal experience and that of other divorced persons I have known, as well as from the experience of those who have tried to be present to their friends or relatives as they went through the divorce process.

Let me add one other word of explanation. My perspective is that of a Christian, specifically a Catholic, woman. Throughout my divorce and my healing from it, I have found my faith to be an important source of strength—both to me and to many of my relatives and friends. Unlike the man at my door, however, it is not my intention to proselytize or push one particular religious point of view. If your religious beliefs are important to you and/or to your friend or relative who is going through a divorce, by all means share it with them—not in any kind of judgmental way, but in a spirit of love. But please do not use religion as a way of putting up a wall or barrier between you and your friend. A person going through a divorce has built enough of them already.

So, if your brother or sister, your son or daughter, your neighbor or friend comes to you one day with the dreaded words, "I'm getting a divorce," don't turn your back or stick your head in the sand. Their problem has just become your problem. You both must help each other survive. Here are ten rules that will help.

RULE I

I had no more excuses. It was Friday night, three months after my former husband had left me. Because it was my mother's bridge night, my father had come to "hang out" with me, although I secretly believed that he had been sent to "babysit" me—the newly jilted daughter.

My baby was asleep, and my father suggested that it was time.

I could think of no more reasons not to, so we headed up to the attic to get boxes to pack the remaining clothes and personal items of my former spouse that I had kept neatly waiting in his dresser drawers in the silent hope that he would someday return.

I had put this off for so long saying that I had no time, no energy. The truth was, I had no desire. As we began to pack, my father moved quickly and quietly. I stopped and asked him why he was in such a hurry.

"If he had stayed, I would have fought like hell to keep him here," Dad said angrily. "But if he's out, he's out."

□□□

It had hardly occurred to me until that moment that my father had been experiencing his own confused emotions over my dissolved marriage. It suddenly made sense to me that he should have to work through his own feelings and work toward some understanding and acceptance of what had happened to him—as well as to his daughter. After all, Dad had also built his own relationship with his son-in-law, a relationship separate and different from mine. That relationship had now disappeared, permanently and unexpectedly. My father needed to mourn a loss, get angry with my former husband, get in touch with how he was going to feel as the father of a divorced woman.

If your friend or relative is going through a separation and divorce, you suddenly have two people you have to worry about. One, obviously, is your friend. He or she needs you to help work through what can be one of the most traumatic of human experiences.

The other person, perhaps not quite so obvious, is you. You, too, have experienced a traumatic event—one that you did not have a direct hand in creating.

Perhaps you were very close to the former spouse. You may have liked, even loved, the person a great deal. You may feel that you have been handed a divorce yourself, one that you neither wanted, asked for, or agreed to. You may even try—and even succeed to some degree—to keep up a separate relationship with that person. But things will never be the same. What was once a couple, a twosome, a pair, a family has become two separate entities, and your life will never return to "normal" again.

Or perhaps you never liked the other person very much. Maybe you just tolerated him or her for the sake of your friend. You might even have always thought that the two of them were wrong for each other. It is possible you feel that the divorce is not such a bad idea, that it is the best solution to an intolerable situation. Doesn't matter. You still have sustained a loss. There has been a major change in your life that you must deal with.

□□□

So, before you can even begin to be helpful to your friend, you must deal with your own emotions. It is normal to feel confused, even torn. You might think your friend is making a mistake. You may feel sorry for the other spouse. Or you may be quite angry at the person who has hurt your friend so much.

You could be relieved that the inevitable has finally happened, or you could have been taken completely, utterly and totally by surprise.

Perhaps you wish you had done something to make things better in their marriage. You find it difficult to sleep at night, pondering the fragility of the institution of marriage or even wondering about your own. If you aren't married, you may decide that you never will.

Your stomach hurts when you run into either your friend or the former spouse unexpectedly in the supermarket. You discover that you can only try to make small talk, or put your foot in your mouth, or start crying yourself.

Other friends and relatives call you up to talk about the situation. You don't know what to say. You don't want to gossip, don't want to violate your friend's confidence, but you also need to talk to someone besides your divorced friend about it.

The key thing to remember about all these emotions is this: they are all right! That's right, they are all right. Emotions are neither good nor bad, neither right nor wrong. They just are. They are your emotions to what has happened to you and to your friend.

If you are angry, it is all right. You might be angry at your friend, or the former spouse, or yourself, or someone else involved in the divorce. Anger is good. Be angry. Punch a wall, yell at the top of your lungs, or have yourself a good cry. You might even need to confront the person you are angry with. That's okay, too. These are your emotions, and you need to deal with them.

You might be sad. Very, very sad. How beautiful that is. Sadness is also good. It means you have lost something precious, or at least your good friend or relative has. Why shouldn't you cry, or feel depressed or wish that none of this had happened?

You will almost certainly be embarrassed. Who wouldn't be? The breakup of a marriage is a very private affair, yet your friend or relative still needs you to get involved in it. It's natural for you to feel a little embarrassed by the whole thing, even though you had nothing to do with it happening. So what if you don't know what to say or do? That's natural. It's how you feel!

You might even be happy. Perhaps your friend has finally gotten up the courage to get out of a dangerous or abusive situation. Maybe theirs was a loveless marriage from the start, or maybe their marriage turned sour because of alcohol or drug abuse or infidelity or workaholism. You might feel that for the first time in many years your friend has a new chance at real happiness. Why wouldn't you be happy? Happy is also good. Be happy! Laugh. Offer a toast to the new situation.

Most probably you will have a mix of emotions. The important thing is that you recognize them, accept them, deal with them for what they are. They are how you feel. Only if you deal with your own emotions will you be able to move on yourself and deal with your friend's divorce, and only after you are able to do that will you be able to help your friend do the same.

□□□

Now that I look back, I can see that those who knew my former husband well seemed mostly to be experiencing varying degrees and stages of grief.

In the early stages of my situation, for example, I saw my father mostly silent and reflective, with occasional grumbling remarks about the divorce. That night we packed my former spouse's belongings, however, I understood that Dad was still angry yet impatient for some closure—thus the importance for him of moving those boxes out of the house.

Not long afterwards, I realized that my sister had finally come out of her stage of denial. "Your husband will come back," she had been telling me since the day he left. "He's just going through a tough time." Time finally helped her come to an acceptance of the situation.

One of my girlfriends struggled with her feelings about the way my former husband had treated me. She sat down and wrote him an angry letter, which she never sent. I could see that this was something she needed to do in order to work through her own emotions.

What I now realize is that In order for my friends and family to be truly understanding and helpful to me, it was necessary for them to deal with their own feelings about my divorce. First of all, it was important for their own process of healing. But it was also important to me that they not repress their own emotions. For them to begin to understand how I felt and be supportive of me, it was important that they were able to do the same for themselves.

□□□

Does all this mean that you need to share all of your feelings about the divorce with your friend right off the bat? Of course not. In many ways, your friend will care less how you feel. His or her feelings will be so overwhelming that they will probably block out any of yours. Most likely, your friend will assume that you feel exactly the same as he or she does. For example, if your friend is sad, you will be assumed to be sad; if he or she is angry, you will be expected to be angry; etc.

It is not necessary for your to share all of your real feelings about the divorce with your friend immediately. Mostly you will be expected to listen and commiserate. But you do need to get in touch with how you really feel. That is why it may be important for you to talk about the divorce with someone other than the friend who is getting divorced. Because the clearer you are about how you feel, the more sympathetic and unemotional you will be able to be with your friend who needs you.

Eventually, your friend will want to know how you feel. If you have dealt with your emotions about the divorce, you will then be able to gently share them with your friend. This will not only help your friend see that he or she is not the only one who has been affected by the divorce, but it will also show him or her that there are a wide range of reactions to the divorce possible and that they can be successfully dealt with.

□□□

On word of caution is in order. You should know that the process of dealing with your emotions will probably go much more quickly for you than for your friend. After all, no matter how close you might have been to the former spouse, you were not on the same level of intimacy and commitment that your friend was. There is no way you can expect him or her to progress as fast as you.

One danger is that once you have successfully dealt with your own feelings about the divorce, you might then want to stop reaching out to your friend. You have come to terms with the divorce. You have worked through your emotions. Why hasn't your friend been able to do the same?

You might find yourself frustrated, for example, to find your friend still angry or depressed when you have already worked through those emotions. Studies have shown, however, that the process of grieving or mourning for a divorced person can take several years, depending on the person and the situation.

Even when they are ready to move on and stop talking about the absent spouse, your friend may need to walk through the stages of grief time and time again. This may get old for you.

Yet this may be when you are most needed!

One young divorced man remembers how much time and energy friends and family gave him immediately following his separation from his wife. "People spent time just sitting with me," he relates. They brought meals while I was very numb. Two months later, however, life went on for them. I felt stranded and helpless and very lonely."

This man knew that for him the work of healing was just beginning. Even though his friends may have worked through their own emotions about the divorce, he still needed them to help him work through his.

Once you have come to grips with the divorce for yourselves, you need to slow down your attempts to rush your divorced friend to do the same. You need to be able to just listen and be present.

□□□

Points to Remember

1. Emotions are neither right nor wrong, they just are.

2. There will be a variety of emotions caused by the divorce of a friend or relative.

3. It is important for you to get in touch with your emotions about the divorce, both for your own peace of mind and so you can be more helpful to your friend.

4. It is not necessary that you share all of your feelings immediately with your friend. You will know when the time has come to do so, and then be sure to do so gently.

5. Your friend may not be able to deal with his or her emotions about the divorce as quickly as you do. Don't drift away or become frustrated when he or she takes time.

RULE 2

*T*he phone rang. During the early, "grieving" days of my separation and divorce, I hated when the phone rang. I always feared the call for "Mr. or Mrs." or the friend or colleague of my former spouse who did not know that he was gone. Most of all, I dreaded that the voice on the other end would be a friend or relative of mine who did not know or had recently found out about...my divorce!

I was in a state of denial at the time. I was so hurt and embarrassed by the divorce that I tried to avoid everyone from my past. I decided (quite unrealistically, of course) that I could change my entire life. I would start over with the few people I trusted. Everyone else who had known me as a married woman would be history.

I did not want others to judge me, pity me or treat me differently. I feared what they would say. Were they surprised? Or, worse yet, had they seen the situation coming? Would they blame me, instead of my former husband? Did they think that I was a failure or a bad person? Would they ask me questions I was not prepared to answer?

My plan was to avoid the world for the rest of my life. But the phone kept on ringing.

One day, it was Sara, an old friend from high school, who had finally heard about my divorce four months after it was final. Her anxiety was evident as she apologized for bothering me, but she wanted to tell me she was sorry about the divorce. After the first few minutes of discomfort on both our parts, Sara and I somehow managed to talk for about forty minutes. We reached a level of intimacy that we had not had in years, and I experienced a wonderful feeling of liberation that night.

Perhaps the people from my past were not my enemies! Maybe they wouldn't all judge me or feel sorry for me or cast me into some "divorced" category.

From then on, things changed for me. I no longer avoided my friends. I was no longer afraid when the telephone rang.

□□□

What impressed me most about Sara's phone call that night was the courage it must have taken for her to reach out to what was really a distant friend. She certainly took a risk. I could have been cold or angry. She had no way of knowing what to expect.

And Sara had no obligation to check up on an old friend with whom she had lost contact. The easy thing would have been to just let it go and not get involved. But she was a compassionate person and a real friend who took a risk to try to help someone who was hurting.

And it made a difference.

The writers of the advertisement to "reach out and touch someone" probably did not have divorced people specifically in mind. It's actually a pretty difficult call to make, for a lot of reasons.

"It's easier said than done," claims one friend of a divorced man.

"Sure I knew that he needed me, and once I got over my own hangup about the situation, I wanted to be there for him. But that first phone call was a tough one. I told myself he didn't want to be bothered; that he probably had enough support from his family already. I thought of every excuse in the book, until I finally just broke down and called him. He was so grateful, I'll never regret it."

□□□

In most cases, it is just too much to ask for the person getting divorced to reach out to others. Your friend's level of discomfort and embarrassment is most likely even higher than yours. Sure, he or she probably has talked with someone else—a best friend, a sibling, a parent, a minister. But often what people need is a variety of friends and relatives to support them.

In the days, weeks and months following a marital breakup, your friend is going to need many and varied messages of affirmation. He or she wants to know that life is going to go on, that friends and relatives have every intention of continuing their relationship, that the divorce has not made him or her a bad or undesirable person.

One of the big needs of recently separated or divorced people is to tell the story of the breakup over and over again. In some ways, it is like the person at the wake who tells the long line of mourners how the deceased died. The repetition of the facts seems to somehow make the whole experience more real.

At this point, what your friend probably needs more than anything is just your presence and willingness to listen. You may hear a lot of anger or see a lot of tears. You may have to hold your friend's hand or put an arm around a shoulder and just assure him or her that everything is going to be all right.

You may hear practical concerns. Where will I live? How will I manage financially? What should I do about the children? You don't need to have all the answers. What your friend needs from you right now is the certainty that you will be there and that you will always be a friend.

□□□

Of course, there are things that you can do right away. One divorced man remembers vaguely the days following his separation. He felt like someone had died because so many people dropped by with food. "It bothered me at the time," he says, "but my friends must have known something I didn't. I see now that I never would have made food for myself. I probably would have gone to a bar by myself to drink if they hadn't come over."

One sister of a newly divorced woman remembers, "My sister was so out of it following her breakup that all she did was sit around and think about her ex-husband. I would ask her if I could do anything to help, but she would always say that everything was fine. Finally, one night I just went over, fed her dog for her, and sat around and watched TV with her. I continued to reach out in this way, and she never seemed angry, so I guess it was okay."

□□□

Newly divorced people, who often have many feelings of inadequacy, sometimes find it difficult to ask their friends for help. "I was so tired and so down," says one woman, "that I really needed help, even if it was something as simple as picking up the groceries or the dry cleaning. What I really needed was a break from my children, but all I could think of was that I had already failed as a wife and didn't want to look like a bad mother too."

Especially in the early stages of your friend's divorce, you need to anticipate needs. When many newly divorced people are asked if they need any help, they say no. They want others to see them as capable of handling the situation.

Very often, too, open-ended offers are not accepted. "Do you need someone to watch the kids?" or "Call me if you need anything" are often ineffective, albeit well-intended.

Try something like this with your friend: "Why don't I come over and hang out with the kids Saturday night so you can grocery shop, take a walk alone or even take a nap?" or "I've got two tickets to the ball game Tuesday night. Let's go."

Even the clearest and most specific offer of help can be refused. It is sometimes hard to distinguish between a refusal based on pride or embarrassment and a genuine desire on the part of your friend to be left alone. Don't give up after only one or two times. You may have to make several offers before your help is accepted.

Not everyone is in a position (or even has the kind of relationship with a divorced person) to stop by with food or offer to babysit. You might need to just touch base with phone calls or remember your friend on holidays or anniversaries. One divorced woman remembers, "I received so many nice cards and letters right after the word got out that I was divorced. I have a special aunt who still sends me cards on important days years later. She knows that I still have my low days."

It may even be that all your offers of friendship and help are rejected. Remember that your friend is going through a traumatic time and may be grieving very deeply. Or he or she may be in a total state of denial about the need for any kind of help at all, claiming that things "have never been better" and "the divorce was the best thing that ever happened to me."

Do not believe your friend. Keep up your presence and your specific offers of help. Eventually, when your friend is ready, your offers will be accepted—or at least appreciated.

□□□

As you continue to reach out to your friend, you may experience all kinds of rejection or denial. One man remembers his mother following her divorce. "At first, she never talked about it at all. We never pushed her, but it seemed really weird that it had been so apparently easy for her to leave my dad. My siblings and I let her know over and over again that we were there for her if and when she needed us. Finally, she shared with us that she had been hoping all along that she and my father would reunite some-how. Meanwhile, my father had moved on with his life and had no intention of returning to her. It took her a long time to come to terms with the whole thing, but I guess everybody must go at his or her own speed."

All friends can do is keep reaching out. Your divorced friend will accept your help if and when he or she is ready. But when he or she is ready, you better be there and not have disappeared be-cause of your own discouragement.

I know that the people who reached out to me made the differ-ence, and I know that they all took a big risk in doing so. Two weeks after my husband left was our wedding anniversary. Two of my girlfriends came over with flowers and Rice Crispy treats. We sat and ate with our kids while it rained outside. Only later did I marvel at their risk in noting my anniversary and trying to celebrate it, but I think that is exactly what I needed that gloomy day.

I don't know how many friends tried to phone me before Sara did, only to get an answering machine or a cold response from me. She was the one who finally broke through, but I thank each and every one of them for trying. I responded when I was ready to respond.

Points To Remember

1. Your friend needs you to keep reaching out. He or she will respond when ready.

2. It is your job to initiate the contacts. It is too much to expect your friend to do it. You have to take the risk of being rejected.

3. Sometimes, especially in the beginning, all your friend needs is a willing listener and a warm hug. You don't have to have all the answers.

4. Your offers of help must be as specific as possible. Take "no" for an answer, but don't hesitate to repeat the offer.

5. Your reaching out must continue for a long time, even years.

RULE 3

I t didn't make any sense to me. I was sad, and she was mad.
A year had passed since my husband had left. It had been a
long year, and my sister bad been a big part of my life. She
cried when he left. She listened when I cried.

And now she was mad.

At me!

"I'm sorry, Mary Kay," she said. "It's just that I'm tired of you
always staying home and moping. You haven't been yourself in
a long time. When we do talk, the conversation always comes
around to your divorce. I'm confused. It seems I can't say anything right. I don't know what to do for you anymore. I can't
seem to say anything that makes a difference...."

My sister was right, of course. I had become a different person.
I did dwell on my divorce. I wasn't myself. But I certainly did not
understand her being mad at me. It didn't make any sense to
me at the time. She, more than anyone, knew how devastated I
was by my divorce. She knew how much I depended on her for
unconditional support. How and why could she be mad at me?

□□□

31

It was only much later that I realized through a serious conversation with my sister that she wasn't mad at me because I was divorced. She was frustrated because my recovery from my divorce was taking so long and she didn't know how to help me move on.

You, too, may find yourself feeling frustrated with your role in your divorced friend's grieving process. You might even find yourself wanting to give up. Please don't. Take heart that your feelings are very typical for the friends and relatives of divorced people.

Your frustration probably comes from a combination of things. You may have a difficult time seeing your loved one in pain or even denial of pain. You want that pain to stop, the sooner the better.

You may be tired of not knowing the right thing to say. One friend explained that even if she had the wisdom of Solomon she was sure that she would make a serious mistake.

You may be disappointed, angry, disgusted. Some friends and family can't stand the inconsistencies of divorced persons who want sympathy but no pity, who claim they want to get on with their lives but remain obsessed with their former spouses.

Many friends want to see immediate results of the work and energy they have put into helping their friends: the interminable phone calls, the frequent visits, the innumerable cards and letters, the hours of hearing the same story over and over again.

□□□

If you have some of these reactions, welcome to the club. Being a friend to a divorced person is no easy task. There are no quick fixes, no secret answers, no sure bets.

Each divorce is unique. The circumstances that occasioned the breakup, the underlying causes of the problem, the personalities of the two partners and their post-divorce relationship, the presence or absence of children and their response, the reactions of families and friends are all different for each couple.

For a man whose wife left him for another, for example, his pain will be one of shame and rejection and loss of trust. A woman who leaves an abusive marriage, on the other hand, may have a mix of feelings: guilt, relief, fear, even joy. A protracted fight over child custody will result in a very different situation from that of a divorced couple who really work together for the good of their children.

And circumstances will change. The wife who is so relieved to leave her husband may have second thoughts when she discovers that he has started dating someone else. Or the person who is so happy to remarry may be in for a shock when the alimony checks stop arriving.

Divorced people, like all people, have their ups and downs. Theirs just seem to be higher and lower than most!

If you are really unlucky, your friend will rebound into the trap of falling in love with another person immediately, perhaps even to the point of remarrying right away. In a few cases, your friend or relative might even get clinically depressed or suicidal.

In all cases, there is only one piece of advice for you: Take one day at a time.

□□□

That's right, take it a day at a time. You've never been prepared for being the friend of a divorced person. You can't be expected to know the rights answers, do the right thing, never make a mistake.

On some days, anything and everything you do or say will be wrong—at least to your divorced friend. He or she is not looking for advice or help or even just a willing ear and shoulder to cry on. It is a punching bag that is wanted or needed, and—guess what?—you're drafted. Sometimes you will be asked (or perhaps not even asked but expected) to bear the brunt of your friends emotions. Your friend may be hurt or angry or frustrated with the former spouse, or the children, or the court system, or relatives, or even himself or herself. But you will be the one that hears all about it.

Think of it as a sign of how much your friend trusts you. You can be dumped on because your friend knows that you love him or her enough to take it without it destroying your relationship.

Here is the truth: Whether he or she admits it or not, your divorced friend needs you. Your divorced friend, even if he or she acts like you are part of the problem, knows that you are the one who is there for him or her. Your friend may not thank you at the time, but eventually your presence and fidelity will be appreciated.

□□□

What can ease your frustration to a certain degree in these circumstances will be the realization and acceptance that you are just taking things one day at a time. One man shared his dilemma at dealing with his brother's divorce. "Some days he wants to curse his ex-wife. Other days he wants to talk about how much he misses her. How am I supposed to know which?"

The answer is that you are not supposed to know. That is impossible, as anyone who has dealt with a divorced friend will attest. You must test the waters, take some risks, but most importantly not take it personally when you make a mistake or are unable to solve your friend's problems.

Remember, it is not your job to rescue or fix your friend. The divorced person must do the work of coming to terms with his or her own life. Your job is mostly just to be present with your friend, offering help when you can and it seems appropriate, taking it one day at a time.

Leunig, a famous Australian cartoonist, depicted this dynamic with a picture of a cat stuck in a tree late at night. Surrounding the tree are bulldozers, cherry pickers and helicopters shining bright lights on the pathetic feline in a feeble attempt to save it. The last part of the cartoon shows the bottom of the tree. Standing there is a man holding a bowl. The caption reads: "Excuse me, but a saucer of milk at the base of the tree works just as well." Your ministry to your friend is not to save. It is to be present, to be patient, to wait, to take things a day at a time.

One brother of a divorced woman remembers how awful it was to wait while watching his sister crawl into a hole following her divorce. She felt responsible in many ways for the divorce, since she had wanted out of the marriage to escape her husband's verbal abuse of herself and their children. She believed that divorce was the only solution, but she did not want to disclose or discuss what she believed was the shame of the situation. She also felt guilty for allowing her children to experience the abuse for so long. She did not want to talk to anyone about the divorce, but her suffering was obvious to her family.

"We weren't sure what to do, since she was obviously pretending there was nothing wrong," her brother relates. "All we could do was continue to be there for her. We persisted in our attempts to get her out of the house once in a while. Eventually, she came around and starting sharing her feelings with us. It wasn't long after that when she agreed to counseling for herself and the kids."

□□□

Many divorced people are reticent at first to talk about the divorce. One divorced man remembers how helpful his family and friends were, even though he found them overbearing at the time. "My mom called me every day following the divorce," he says. "She said she just wanted to talk, but I was sure she was checking up on me. My sister was always stopping by and suggesting outings. I felt insulted at first, as though I was the pity case of the family. Then one day, Mom was too busy to call. I realized then how much I anticipated and needed my family's support. I started calling them."

One daughter worried about how to be supportive of her father while not betraying her mother after they divorced. "I didn't fall all over him, trying to pick him up. But I do remember dropping hints that I would do whatever he needed. I called him every day. Sometimes he would want to be left alone. Other times he would repeat stories and anxieties I had heard the day before."

Many friends and family members have no qualms about pursuing a divorced person with phone calls, visits and cards. Even they, however, sometimes become frustrated with the response...or lack thereof.

"I got so tired of the tears," one woman confessed. "I found myself finding excuses not to call my friend, since I knew that we would only talk about the divorce. I was angry with her for allowing her selfishness to interfere with our friendship."

All friends and family can do is remind themselves that "it won't always be this way," even if it is also true that "things will never be the same again." Taking it one day at a time is the only solution.

□□□

Friendships that survive the turmoil of a divorce often reach a new depth of vulnerability, commitment and love. The potentially destructive situation for a friendship brought about by the divorce can also bring growth to both individuals and to their relationship.

For example, I was never closer to my sister than when we were going through my divorce together. Even when she got mad at me, I realized that it was because she loved me and wanted what was best for me.

Much doubt often fills the mind of the friend of a divorced person. You doubt that your friend will ever deal successfully with the divorce, you doubt that your relationship will ever withstand the tension you are experiencing, you doubt if there will ever be a time when the tears or the anger or the bitterness will subside.

You can count on a few things if you stick in there. You will be frustrated with your friend many times. You will feel pain yourself as you watch your friend struggle with his or her sometimes overwhelming emotions. Your relationship will undoubtedly change—often for the better, sometimes for the worse.

All you can do is take things one day at a time. Your presence will be your gift. With faith and prayers and patience you may one day come to the point where things begin to get better. One mother of a divorced woman recalls a day when she and her daughter finally broke through the pain of her divorce. "I remember, in the midst of our daily phone call, my daughter exclaiming, 'Mom, I just realized something. I didn't cry once yesterday. Can you believe it? I forgot to cry!' We laughed so hard, mostly in joy that we had both finally seen the light at the end of her long divorce tunnel. I was so happy for her, and I was especially glad that I had stayed with her through it all. I was thankful that I had held her hand, even on the days when she had struggled so to make me let it go."

Points to Remember

1. Being a friend to a divorced person is not easy.

2. Your presence is the most important gift you can give to your friend.

3. Your friend may not always be receptive to you. Don't use that as an excuse to stay away.

4. You will make lots of mistakes while trying to support your friend or relative through a divorce. Each divorce is unique, don't expect to have all the answers.

5. All this might make your relationship stronger, better, deeper.

RULE 4

Mostly, I just felt angry. I remember very clearly the look on the face of my friend at work when I asked if someone was having a baby shower for Sandy, a girl who worked in our office. My friend didn't want to answer, since the shower was on the next Saturday and she knew I had not been invited.

"Oh, Mary Kay, we didn't want you to feel like you had to buy a gift for the baby," she finally blurted out nervously. "We know that you are going through rough financial times right now with the divorce and all...."

Although I knew my friend was trying to make me feel better, I suddenly felt very bad all over. It was as though I had been knocked on the head with a hammer as a loud, booming voice bellowed from the sky, "YOU ARE DIVORCED. YOU ARE DIF-FERENT NOW, AND EVERYONE KNOWS IT."

"We thought you might not be ready to be around everyone since it's still so early," my friend continued. "We were only thinking about you."

So not only were all my friends from work getting together with-

out me, but I had not even been allowed the right to decide for myself what would be best for me.

I suddenly wondered who I was. How did people perceive me? How did I think about myself? What was my new "identity" as a divorced woman? Would there ever be a time when the word "divorce" would not silently accompany how people thought about me, how I thought about myself?

□□□

I couldn't say for sure—even today—how I would have responded if I had been invited to that party. I know my friends were just trying to protect me. They were right that I was embarrassed by my new identity as a divorced person, and they were also correct that I didn't have much money for gifts at the time.

But I was angry with them then, and I remain angry with them now (although I forgive them). Rather than help me accept and begin to live with my new identity, my friends had left me in nowhere land—no longer married, not really single, unready and unable to function in my new role.

Sure, it might have been a little uncomfortable for a few minutes at the shower. Yes, I might have had to scrounge around for a gift. But I had to do all that eventually anyway. My friends could have helped me, instead of making me feel that there was something wrong with me.

□□□

Quite possibly, you have already experienced a similarly awkward moment with your friend or relative who is going through a divorce. He or she may not have reacted with anger. It may have been sorrow or depression or self-loathing. A clear understanding of your friend's state of mind about his or her identity will be helpful to you as you try to help.

First, you must keep in mind that divorce will most often cause a person to develop a very low self-esteem. (This may not be the case when people have left abusive situations, although they are still likely to feel down because they did not act sooner.)

People going through separation and divorce experience a variety of different emotions: relief, anger, sadness, guilt, shock, fear and more. But no matter what their feelings, one fact is universal and incontrovertible: Where once they were half of a team, part of a couple, the spouse of another, now they are not.

Now they are "newly single," a "divorcee," a "single parent," a "former spouse." Worse yet, they are—or are perceived to be— "a loser," "lonely," "sad," "troubled," "depressed," etc., etc.

Especially if the marriage lasted for several years, this new "identity" can be terrifying. Very few people enter marriage anticipating or expecting divorce. In fact, just the opposite is true. The wedding is "the happiest day" of their lives and they promise to remain married "until death do us part." Divorce, on the other hand, is viewed as a real failure and is even condemned by some as immoral and against their religious beliefs.

Divorce can make people feel like a balloon that is suddenly popped. Many people go along with their identity tied to their marriage. When that marriage finally breaks apart—whether suddenly or not—their healthy sense of self can disappear with it.

Such sudden and often very low drop in self-esteem can promote some very unhealthy behavior in your divorced friend. Some run away and try to isolate themselves from others, especially those who knew them as half of a marriage. Others delve into extremes of sexual promiscuity, over-eating or drinking, or an intensified work load. Some even turn to religion in an unhealthy and dependent way. The well-known phenomenon of "rebounding" into another relationship is often the result of a recently divorced person attempting to regain his or her sense of self-worth and attractiveness.

□□□

Even though some of the methods divorced people adopt to deal with their low self-esteem seem to make them happy, many of their strategies often actually postpone the necessary development of their new identities.

This is where you come in. You need to encourage the development of your friend's true new identity. This will obviously depend on what stage of the divorce process your friend or relative is in, his or her personality and personal circumstances, and— most importantly—your relationship.

You cannot develop your friend's new identity for him or her, but you can help. Merely acknowledging that things have changed is important. If your friend continues to talk about the former spouse, for example, you might jokingly ask, "Who?" Get your friend down to the bank to open a new checking account, change the name on the front doorbell, put away some of the old family photos with the two of them together.

Sometimes it is your role as a friend to encourage the person to seek professional help. He or she may really need to see a counselor or minister to help them through the crisis. Lawyers, accountants, doctors, dentists all need to be informed of the situation and sometimes new ones need to be found. You can help by encouraging your friend to pick up the phone and make an appointment. You may even have to drive or go along.

You might also be helpful with any children your friend might have. Perhaps they need someone other than their father or mother to talk to about their own and their parents' identities. They might need someone to help inform their teachers or coaches or employers that things have changed. Sometimes, the best thing you can do is to offer to babysit for the children while your friend goes and tries out his or her new identity.

This raises an interesting question about encouraging your friend to socialize or even date after the divorce. The word here is caution. Please do not try to set your newly divorced friend up with that single friend you've always thought would make a good spouse or, even worse, your other newly divorced friend or relative. Remember that it takes literally years to recover from most divorces. The last thing your friend needs is to try to recover his or her self-esteem through a new relationship. When your friend is truly ready, you might encourage a little socializing, but don't push your friend to get serious about another relationship for a long time.

There are many groups for divorced and separated people and for single parents. You might check one out and suggest it to your friend at the right time. A call to a local church or synagogue should result in a few recommendations.

You might also encourage your friend to turn to prayer and religion as a help. If he or she is active in a congregation already, encourage that. If not, invite your friend to join you at your house of worship or suggest that the two of you find one together.

Finally, you should encourage your friend to establish a new identity at work. Bosses and colleagues need to be informed of the situation. If your friend is unable to become comfortable with his or her new identity at work (if, for example, the former spouse also works there), then you should encourage a search for new employment.

The most important thing to remember is that you need to encourage your friend to accept his or her new identity in every phase of life. Your friend is separated or divorced. That is not going to change. Things are not going to go back to the way they were. Your job is to help your friend realize and accept that fact without feeling that he or she is somehow less of a person for it.

□□□

One man said that for the first three years following his divorce he felt totally alienated from others. One woman at work said to him, "I don't know how anyone could get a divorce. People who get divorced are quitters."

It wasn't until his friends started to make him accept his new identity as a divorced person who was still loved by many that he knew he wasn't a quitter and could be a complete person again. He said that he only wished it hadn't taken them three years.

If my friends had invited me to Sandy's baby shower, I could have said yes or no for myself. Whatever my answer, however, it would have been one step forward in establishing my new identity.

You can play a very important role in your friend's process of establishing a strong, healthy, new identity. You can make a difference mostly through your presence and your patience and your unflinching hold on reality.

Realize that your identity has now changed also. Now, perhaps for the first time, perhaps for the tenth, part of your identity is "friend (or relative) of a divorced person." You need to accept this new identity also, for by doing so you will help your friend do the same.

Points to Remember

1. Your friend will most likely experience a loss of self-esteem after the divorce. Remind your friend that he or she is still loved and lovable.

2. Your friend or relative needs to accept his or her new identity as a divorced person.

3. Your job is not to protect your friend from this new identity but to encourage him or her to get on with life.

4. Try to be of specific help to your friend in establishing his or her new identity. Pick up a phone. Check something out. Go with your friend on a first visit.

5. You now have a divorced friend. Your identity has now changed also, no matter how slightly. Accept it and work within it.

RULE 5

I was crying again. Only this time, the tears came from laughter. It was the first time I had laughed that hard since my former husband left me.

My girlfriend had showed me a card she had bought for my former spouse. She had paid $1.75 for it.

The cover of the card was decorated with flowers all around the edge. The print was beautiful and bold: "JESUS LOVES YOU." When you opened the card, it read: "The rest of us think you're a jerk!"

We laughed and laughed when we thought of my former husband reading the card. Revenge was sweet! Our tears were strangely refreshing.

□□□

My friend had no intention of mailing the card, of course. The point was not to make my former husband feel badly, it was to make me feel better.

Jean de La Bruyère once wrote: "Life is a tragedy for those who feel, and a comedy for those who think." It's no great secret that divorce is usually tragic for the couple, their children, their families and friends. It's tragic partly because everyone feels so strongly about it. There are feelings of tension, pain, sadness, anger, embarrassment, depression, and sometimes even those of acceptance, relief, peace.

The tragic element of the divorce process is to be expected. In a sense, the emotions involved are easy to get in touch with. Divorced people must work through their feelings if they are to successfully recover from their divorce and move on with their lives. As a friend of relative of a divorced person, you will be asked or expected to participate in your fair share of tragedy.

This sense of tragedy, however, can get to the point where it overwhelms everyone involved. A fine line exists between "good grief" and "bad grief." The grieving process of divorce, necessary as it is, cannot be allowed to become a bottomless pit—one sad day upon the next, each one sadder than the day before.

Relief or escape from the blues eventually becomes a necessity for every divorced person, and part of your job as his or her friend is to provide some comic relief.

□□□

Though it may feel awkward at first, humor can be cleansing, relieving and healing. The "thinking" part of comedy, as Bruyère implied, is that laughter appeals more to the head than to the heart.

I remember coming across a quotation by Woody Allen in a magazine that went something like this: "For a while my wife and I pondered whether to take a vacation or get a divorce. We decided to get the divorce. A trip to Bermuda is over in two weeks, but a divorce is something you always have with you." My laughter was not strong, in fact it was strangely bittersweet. But I did feel some of the sadness that had been there for a very long time fall from my mood.

Even though some people are natural improvisational comedians and there is a place for the quick quip or comeback, you mostly have to plan out your humor with your divorced friend. You must think about the best way and time to try being funny and how your friend might react.

It's not a real good idea, for example, to make jokes when the separation or divorce first happens. Telling your friend that "we'll both laugh about this later," may not sit too well with someone who has just lost their partner for life and the other parent of their children. Joking in front of the children may not be a good idea, either. Remember, kids don't always take things the same way adults do.

You also need to be careful not to let the humor get to the point where your divorced friend uses it to avoid the reality of his or her situation. Some people use humor as a defense mechanism, and that can be counterproductive.

Do not, for example, allow your friend to put himself or herself down all the time. "Don't ask me to decide," your friend might say. "I obviously have poor judgment. Look at the person I chose to marry." That might be funny once, but not twice.

Making fun of the former spouse might be hilarious, but it can quickly turn dark and bitter. It may be humorous to compare the former spouse to Donald Duck or Count Dracula, but it may not be the best way to help your friend escape negative feelings from the divorce.

The humor you need to introduce back into your friend's life has to be aimed at his or her mind. Your friend needs to begin gently to see the absurdity or silliness or even futility of his or her situation.

□□□

Sometimes the first funny comment will come from your divorced friend. One woman remembers asking her sister, about a year after the sister's divorce, where she had gotten the book sitting on the coffee table title, *Love: A Lifetime Commitment*. Her sister replied, "It was one of your wedding gifts to us!" Rather than feeling embarrassed by the situation, the two woman laughed. "We probably should try to get some money back on it," the woman told her sister.

Another divorced man remembers stopping by his parents' house after church. "For some strange reason, my mother asked me where I had sat in church," he says. "I told her that I was of course in the section where all the divorced people had to sit with big 'Ds' on their foreheads. Mom gave me a strange look and then we both laughed."

Mostly, however, it will be your job to initiate the comedy. Of course you will make mistakes. What are apologies for? But, on the other hand, if you don't make your friend laugh again, who will?

I remember about six months after my divorce receiving a funny card from my aunt that made my day. It had been a long day at work, my baby had a bad cold, and I was dead tired. I was definitely not in a "funny" mood.

I opened my aunt's card, which read on the cover: "Whenever I am feeling down, I run out in the yard and dance and spin and jump around and around." The inside of the card said: "Then I run and throw up on the shoes of someone I don't like." I laughed for a long time and then went to bed in a much better mood. The next day, I had a reason to call my aunt, and I could start out on a light mood with her by thanking her for the card and telling her how much it meant to get it.

I remember a note dropped in my mailbox by a colleague at work. He had simply put his initials under a quotation he had found: "Never get married while you're going to college; it's hard to get a start if a prospective employer finds you've already made one mistake."

His note gave me a smile, but it also broke the ice between us about the divorce. Later, I was able to talk to him more openly and seriously about my situation than I had before he sent the note.

□□□

Sometimes the laughter comes only after time has passed and you and your friend can view the entire divorce experience in perspective. It's not so much the joke or the funny card that provides the humor, it is the entire situation. My family still makes fun of the way I literally cried into the gravy bowl during grace at dinner the Christmas after my divorce, which everyone at the time pretended not to notice. It may have taken until August of the next year before we could all laugh at "the Grinch that ruined Christmas," but I truly believe that the laughter we all were able to share made some of my pain go away.

Your humor might be based on the awkward situations that divorced people are constantly faced with. If you are with your friend when you accidently encounter his or her former spouse out with a fantastic date, there are two ways you can react—with tragedy or with comedy. The tragic approach (which may, of course, be the appropriate one) would be to let your friend cry or get angry or become depressed.

Another approach, however, might be to jokingly suggest that the two of your go outside, find the former spouse's car, and let the air out of the tires!

You are the friend, you have got to judge the best course of action. The rule is, however, to keep humor alive. If your friend is to truly recover from the divorce, he or she is somehow going to have to let laughter back into his or her life. You can help.

I'm glad my friend did not send that nasty card to my former husband, but I'm sure glad she showed it to me!

Points to Remember

1. Divorce is tragedy, but it can also at times be comedy.

2. Your friend needs you to help keep humor alive. Look for the humor in the situation.

3. You are the judge of what and when humor is appropriate. You will make mistakes, but you need to risk them.

4. Monitor your humor around the children. Remember that they won't always understand it.

5. Don't let your friend's humor become self-deprecating or mean-spirited.

RULE 6

CHANGE YOUR CALENDAR

The baby tiger toddled in front of me, giggling with glee. I, in contrast, struggled to smile. Halloween night on the year following my divorce was (surprisingly to me, at least) the most difficult day of that year.

I remember how terrible I felt as I took my one-year-old son to a friend's house to trick-or-treat. Everybody commented on his painted-on tiger whiskers and cute little tiger ears. I was excited for his delight over the festivities, because I remembered how much I enjoyed this day as a child.

My excitement dwindled, though, as I watched husbands and wives beaming together over the energy in the air that night. I had always liked the traditional division of labor in our area on Halloween: the moms stayed home and passed out the treats, and the dads took the children around the neighborhood. Now I had to do both.

I had placed a tiger costume on my little boy and a plastic smile on my face and gone out into the world. "I'm doing okay, everybody!" my actions fairly shouted. But deep inside, I felt that even though time kept moving I would never catch up...because I was divorced.

That first year, on October 31, I winced as I thought about how many more holidays and birthdays and anniversaries were around the bend.

□□□

That Halloween night, I made a vow to myself. I was not going to let my divorce destroy my own and my child's celebration of special days and anniversaries. What surprised me was how much help I needed from my friends and relatives to keep that vow.

The year following a divorce is filled with "marriage residue." Whether your divorced friend mentions them or not, the many "landmark" days during the year push an instant-replay button. Divorced people start an inner dialogue which can often be quite painful:

"Where was I a year ago today?"

"Don't you remember? On this day every year, you and your former spouse used to go to a certain place with the same people and did those special things?"

"Now I remember. I wonder if those same people are still getting together without me? I wonder if my former spouse even remembers what we used to do...or maybe is still doing it with someone else? I wonder if the kids remember? I wonder how I should deal with them about this? Should we start a new tradition? Should we continue the old tradition? How will I feel if I do? What will I say? How will I act? What will others think?"

"Better face the music. You're divorced, you know."

"Thanks for nothing."

□□□

These unspoken dialogues—which are really monologues with the divorced person speaking both parts—vary as divorced people deal with their divorces. Sometimes the memories will be good, but bittersweet. Other times, the memories might be painful and filled with regret. They often include goals that the couple had hoped to attain but never did because of the divorce.

Each spring, for example, one man remembers that he was in the process of attaining his master's degree when his marriage fell apart. He dropped the courses he was taking at the time and hasn't returned, but the first buds of spring bring back the memory of his failure.

One single mother shared how devastated she had been on Mother's Day the year following her divorce. "My children were so young that they didn't know they should recognize the day. If my former husband had been around, he would have taken them to buy a card or fix me breakfast in bed or something."

Another woman remembers a major project she and her former husband had started, never to be complete. "The dream house we were going to build would have been done in September," she explains. "We had just bought the land when he left me." Now, each Labor Day is also an occasion for regret for that dream that will never be realized.

Divorced people will not all name the same day or days as the most difficult to handle. For some, it might be Christmas or New Year's or Passover, for others it is a birthday or a wedding anniversary or the day of the split-up. Some find vacations the hardest to handle, while others hate Thanksgiving or some other family-oriented holiday. Many remember specific events—both good or bad—from the marriage itself: the day the divorce was finalized, an infidelity discovered, a honeymoon taken. Special dates involving children—births, first communions, first days of school, for example—are especially difficult.

My own family were surprised when I informed them how difficult Halloween had been for me. The day had never been especially significant to any of us, but it suddenly stood out for me.

□□□

Part of the job of being a friend to a divorced person is to change your own calendar to reflect important or difficult days in your friend's new life, and then to make sure that you are sensitive to how your friend might be feeling.

The adjustments that need to be made are almost overwhelming at times. When you stop to consider that your friend or relative might have spent many years building a life with his or her former spouse, however, you will realize how deep-seated and pervasive the problem is. Whether the divorce was wanted or not, whether it is ultimately a good thing for your friend or not, the annual calendar of memories will be full and often painful.

You, as the friend or family member, may not need much convincing regarding the changes that have taken place. You might also be experiencing the residual effects of the broken relationship. The change in your friend's life may also be creating uncomfortable changes in yours.

Holidays whose greatest dilemma used to be "Who is bringing the rolls?" now become "Will the children be with you or your former spouse this year?" Weddings that used to symbolize only love and happiness now involve complex pew seating arrangements and tense negotiations over the taking of photographs.

New traditions need to be formed to fill the voids created by the divorce. If your divorced relative or friend used to stop over every Sunday afternoon with the kids, for example, it may have to be changed to Thursday nights to accommodate new custody arrangements. You may have to move the exchange of Christmas or Hanukkah gifts to the night before or the morning after you used to do it.

You need to try to help make these changes as painless as possible. One daughter of newly divorced parents recalls how hard it was for her to decide where she should go for Christmas dinner. "I was miserable that first year, but I realized how miserable they were, too. I told myself that we could all keep on being miserable every Christmas for the rest of our lives or we could accept the new reality and make it work. I will say this much: It was much easier for both them and me when we all agreed to accept a hectic Christmas with two dinners rather than all sitting around resenting the divorce."

□□□

A new, revised calendar will identify for you not only the significant, universally recognized holidays that might affect your divorced friend or relative but also the specific dates that might only matter to him or her.

Sit down with your calendar and mark down—from the best of your memory—those days that might be important to your friend: birthdays, anniversaries, key dates related to the marriage or the divorce. Note also when there will be major changes in your friend's life: the first day the kids will stay overnight with the former spouse, the day the divorce will become final, the day your friend's former spouse remarries. Be aware when your friend's daily routine changes: the first day the kids go back to school, a new job, a move to a new home.

These days would be excellent opportunities for you to make your presence and support felt through a visit, a phone call or a greeting card. One divorced man never received an Easter card in his life. "The year I was divorced," he relates, "I received five. It felt great to know that people were still that concerned for me even several months after my divorce. It made it easier to get through a tough day."

It is not necessary that you mention the divorce in these encounters. As a matter of fact, it is probably better most of the time not to bring it up. Your friend will know why you are concerned and will be thankful for it. Neither of you need to acknowledge the fact that it might be a painful time.

Sometimes, of course, it will come up. Your greeting or contact might trigger the memory or the emotion that your friend has been trying to repress or ignore. You need to be prepared to listen and console and maybe cheer up your friend. Keep in mind, however, that while your support will most certainly ease your friend's pain, it will not erase it.

You may even wonder sometimes what difference you make as you sit with a very sad person in the middle of holiday festivities. Your friend might not seem to be very energized by your visit. Your presence, however, might be the difference between your friend sitting alone in that gloom and sitting in the gloom with a friend.

□□□

The day your divorced friend can say, "A year ago, I was starting my life over," will be another day worth noting on your own calendar.

The second Halloween after my divorce was better than the first, partly because my family and friends were aware of how difficult the day was for me. Some of them made sure that they came over and helped me dress my son and hand out candy. The third Halloween was better than the second, and now I can even enjoy the holiday again.

The first year following a divorce is, in a strange way, like a first baby's first year. The mother and father who are keeping a baby book watch for the "firsts" like a hawk: the first smile, the first word, the first steps, the first tooth. After that first year is over, most parents will tell you it is harder to concentrate on every first for that first child—and even more difficult to note all the key events for their next children.

The same is true for you and your divorced friend or relative. The first year after the divorce will be the toughest and it is that year when you will be needed most. Most divorced people can acknowledge at least one monumental landmark positively: the day that their "firsts" are "firsts" no longer.

Points to Remember

1. The year is full of holidays, anniversaries and special dates relating to the marriage and divorce that will affect your friend or relative.

2. You need to mark your own holiday and anniversary calendar to remind yourself of your friend's special dates, especially during the first year following the divorce.

3. You do not necessarily need to mention the divorce when you contact your friend on special dates, but you also should be prepared for his or her reaction.

4. Although your presence will ease your friend's pain, it cannot erase the pain.

5. The first year following the divorce will end eventually and things will get easier, but you will still need to be sensitive to your friend's feelings and situation.

RULE 7

It was Mother's orders. She told me to get out of the house for a while so she could "move things around." I suppose that in my state of mind after my divorce, she could have replaced everything in the house and I wouldn't have noticed.

I went on a long walk, returning twenty-five minutes later.

At first I wasn't sure what she had done, but I knew that things felt different. I noticed a few chairs moved, a vase on a different table, a pile of books restacked in a different order. Then I noticed the big change: the missing photographs and a missing wedding album. I looked at her.

"I didn't throw them away," she explained. "I just moved them for now. You need to move on, and so do I."

□□□

My mom, of course, was right. Not only did I need to move on, but so did she.

The reason we don't move on, of course, is that change is painful. To move on means to accept that our lives have changed, probably forever. It means coming to grips with the fact that things will never be the same again. It means accepting and even mourning the loss of "what was" and even "what might have been."

Moving on also means facing our biggest fear: the fear of the unknown. We really do not know what our lives will be like in the future. If we did, we probably would not be so hesitant to embrace change. But the fear of the unknown is closely tied to our fear of the ultimate unknown—death—and so we are usually not eager to encounter it.

□□□

For divorced people, the fear of the unknown is magnified by what they have just experienced. Not only have they lost the person with whom they had vowed to face the unknown "until death do us part," but they might also have been betrayed (or betrayed themselves) the trust they had placed in another. Now they are being expected to face the future by themselves and on their own, and to trust again that things will work out well—even though they have not to this point.

That is why you need to be there for your friend or relative, insisting that you both must continually move forward and promising that you, at least, are worthy of trust and will not abandon him or her.

Ask friends of any divorced person what the hardest task is in helping their friend. They will most likely answer, "To keep from getting stuck." They will tell you of the pain on the face of their divorced friend as he or she is forced to make change after change to get to a different place, a different stage, a different state of mind. It is one of your jobs to be the source of strength for your divorced friend—to support him or her in moving on or even to jump in with a friendly shove when it is needed.

No matter how painful a change may seem, more often than not it is an essential step to "getting better." Most divorced people will get stuck from time to time in various stages of denial or grief or anger. They will wallow in certain habits or moods that are counterproductive. This is normal. It is kind of like watching a car spinning its wheels in the mud—the driver knows what is happening but doesn't know what else to do. Only when an outsider comes along and pours some sand under the wheels and gives a push can the car get moving again.

One divorced woman remembers how much she appreciated the help of friends and family members as she moved out of the house in which she and her former husband had lived for twelve years. "I don't know what I would have done if my friends and mom and dad had not packed everything for me. It was an almost impossible task for me to physically move twelve years of memories into boxes."

It's not always a matter of encouraging change, either. Sometimes you need to counsel stability. A brother remembers his sister calling him to tell him that her husband and she were getting divorced: "She was babbling on about how she was going to move far away with the kids. She was going to get the next plane to leave for Virginia so that she wouldn't have to be near her former husband. All I could think was that she had a good job here and that her children would need the stability of their present friends, schools and home while they were experiencing the disruption of the divorce. I finally talked her into waiting a month before making such momentous decisions. She never did move."

□□□

The right movements in divorce situations can be very different, depending on the persons and the circumstances. Sometimes, it may be clear and simple: the divorced person must move out of a house or apartment, for example. Or perhaps, as in the case above, the person should stay put.

Other times, the movement needed is less clear and more complex. You friend might need to move from unhealthy to healthy behavior or habits. One woman remembers driving her friend home from a bar after a wild night of drinking. "I felt that was the perfect time for me to comment on the hectic pace that she had been keeping after divorcing her high school sweetheart," the woman explains. "She reacted very negatively, but later admitted that I had been right."

Another divorced man was clearly ignoring his children, who were living with his former wife. One of his friends had to intervene and confront the man on his actions. "I told him that these were still his kids and always would be," the man relates. "I told him that he had to stop feeling sorry for himself, pull himself together, and become the best damn divorced dad any kid ever had."

The reality may be that occasions may arise in which your friend becomes totally stuck, as evident by severe mood changes, extreme behavior, or clinical depression.

One woman remembers observing her cousin remain in bed for days on end. "The divorced came as a great surprise to her," the woman relates. "She was so depressed that she chose her bed as the great escape. Because I was in the best situation to do so of anybody in the family, I moved in with her for a few months to help around the house. Mostly, I was there to kick her out of bed. 'Honey, I'm home,' I'd scream when I got back from work. I tried to make her laugh and face the fact that she had to move on with her life."

Another man confronted his friend with his self-destructive behavior: "I told him his house was a mess, his eating habits were awful and his attitude toward his career was stupid. I honestly think he felt relieved that someone noticed his world was crumbling and insisted that he change."

□□□

One important way of moving forward in cases like these is to recommend that your friend seek professional counseling. He or she may resist, either arguing that "things aren't that bad" or being too immobilized to act. Your friend might even be so convinced that there is a stigma to seeing a counselor that he or she resists or refuses to do so. There is probably little use in trying to force the issue, but you can continue to hold out the idea.

You may be able to show your friend, with a gentle nudge, that the remedy of professional counseling may be temporarily uncomfortable but essential in the long run. In these cases, you may have to find a counselor for your friend, drive your friend to the first couple of appointments, or even offer to pay the fee for the first sessions.

One divorced woman remembers her counseling as extremely draining: "I was forced to look at parts of me I didn't want to look at but really needed to. One session, my counselor was able to show me that a planned 'reunion' with my husband to discuss some financial questions would only bring me back to the terrible state I had been in for the previous three years. It makes sense now that I needed counseling, but at the time I needed my family and friends to push me to do it."

Not all divorce situations are extreme or require professional help, of course. You might want to suggest group counseling or a support group to your friend. Many churches, synagogues and social service agencies sponsor such groups. On the other hand, you might need only to take a friend out to lunch, write a note, or remove a few photographs from a room to help you friend keep on moving on.

You are the person in the best position to measure what your friend needs, and—guess what—you still may be wrong! But the potential payoff is worth the risk you take. If you make a mistake or suggest a bad strategy, you friend will forgive you. But if you don't speak up, don't offer to help, don't confront your friend when necessary, you are not doing the job you are needed to do.

The important thing is that you insist that your friend keep moving forward. It is the difference between sitting in the mud, spinning your wheels, or getting the traction needed to get out of the rut.

□□□

Here's the other thing about moving on: You need to move on as well. If you insist on remaining stuck where you are, you are not going to be very helpful to either your friend or yourself.

Sometimes it can be family and friends who hold a divorced person back. If, after a decent interval of mourning the loss of a marriage, for example, your friend begins to date again, you do neither of you any good to try to hold him or her back. Under the guise of trying to "do what is best" for your friend or to "keep someone from being hurt," you may in fact be holding your friend (and yourself) from making the changes necessary to move forward.

This can be true for any kind of change your friend or relative needs to make. Perhaps he or she really does need to move to get away from (or even to be closer to for the sake of the children) the former spouse. Are you standing in the way because of your own feelings and needs or out of genuine concern for your friend or relative?

Maybe you friend wants to change the way holidays are celebrated in order to move on from painful memories of the way things were. Are you the one insisting that things need to remain the same?

The main point to remember is that it is not only your friend who needs to let go of the past and embrace the future. So do you. The sooner you realize that you both need to always move forward, the sooner you both will do so.

My mother moved the furniture and removed the photos to help me, to be sure. But she also needed to do so for herself.

Points to Remember

1. Change is difficult for all of us because of our fear of the unknown.

2. Your divorced friend or relative is facing the future without the partner he or she planned for and after trust has been broken at least once.

3. Your friend needs you to keep insisting that he or she keep moving forward, even if your advice is sometimes unwelcome.

4. Sometimes the best help you can give to your friend is to suggest professional help.

5. You also need to keep moving forward and not allow your own fears and uncertainties to get you stuck.

RULE 8

I tried to read the story in a fun and cheery manner for my little boy, because he loves silly voices. But I was amazed at how happy I sounded and how miserable I felt. "And the Little Engine shouted its song, 'I think I can, I think I can' over and over again. Its wheels struggled to keep on track while it puffed and chugged along."

I had just gotten off the phone with a mutual friend of my ex-husband and mine. She had "kindly" told me news of my former spouse's involvement with another woman for the past several months. Had I known? No, I had not.

Up until then, I had felt that I had progressed a great deal lately in establishing a stronger foundation of self esteem and a new game plan for my future, but this news floored me. What had begun to make sense before the phone call had once again become a blur. I was back to peg one. All of the steps I had made forward were suddenly non-existent.

As I read my son his story, I began to hear a chant enter my mind that I had not heard for a long time: "I don't think I can, I'm sure I can't...."

□□□

Boom! Bam! That may be the sound you hear on occasion as your divorced friend or relative hits a brick wall without notice.

These walls are solid. Not imagined. Don't believe otherwise.

They may be caused by news of the former spouse's new relationship or success, a setback in divorce proceedings, the negative reaction of one of the children. Or they may be caused by something as simple as an object pulled from a junk drawer that brings back a memory too overwhelming to handle.

Setbacks in the divorce process are as unique as divorces themselves. The only thing you can say for sure about them is that they will happen.

My friend Pete Gepson wrote this poem about setbacks, called "Cycles II":

> The ache at last
> Seems to subside.
> My sighs turned to surprise.
> My life blood had not joined it
> As it slowly faded.
>
> The numbness gave way to
> A tingling,
> A feeling of quiet excitement.
> The dandelions
> Again became my friends,
> The night
> No longer my enemy.
>
> Then
> Swiftly, as if with a vengeance,
> It returned.
> Out of nowhere
> It blindsided me.
> That sickening emptiness.
> Aching.
> It continues to cycle.

The result of these setbacks is that they paralyze the divorced person. Whether for an hour, a week, a month, a year or forever, setbacks will pull your divorced friend back to what may seem like the beginning of the entire sorry story. Your friend or relative, who has finally begun to feel better and hopeful, will lose ground and panic.

One divorced woman remembers how she felt the day her son told her that his dad, the man she had been married to for seventeen years and from whom she had been separated for only five months, was planning to get married as soon as the divorce was final. "I thought I was going to throw up," she recalls. "I knew that our marriage was not the most healthy thing for me or my children, and I never wanted a reconciliation. I had come to a certain peace about the whole thing. I hadn't even been to see my counselor in several weeks because things were getting so much better. I was starting to get used to and like the new me, but when my son told me the news, I felt worse than the day we parted. I called my counselor the next day, and we started all over again."

□□□

Although they are always a surprise, setbacks should not be unanticipated. They will happen to your friend, and you need to be ready to help when they do.

For example, we talked earlier about changing your own holiday and anniversary calendar to reflect what might be going on in your friend's life. It doesn't take a genius to guess that your friend might react strongly to his or her next wedding anniversary after the divorce. You could be waiting at that wall already— either waving your friend off or at least being on the scene when the crash takes place!

One man remembers how unproductive he was at his job about

three months after his separation. "I'm the kind of person who writes everything down in his calendar," he explains. "One day I came into work and saw on my daily planner, 'Graduation! Have a party!' It took me a minute to realize that I had written this date down months before my wife and I separated. I had supported her all the way through college and then she had left me just before she finished. I might as well have stayed home from work for all I got done the next few days."

In this case, none of the man's family or friends anticipated or even knew that he had had a setback. But they might have known. Most of them were quite aware that the wife had in fact graduated. They knew the story of how he had supported her in her studies for years. If one of them had called the man on the day—to commiserate, to invite him out for dinner, to joke about all the money the man would save from not having to put his former wife through graduate school—he might have weathered the setback a little better.

□□□

Usually, it is new situations that bring about the greatest shocks. One woman remembers the first wedding she attended following her divorce. "No divorced person forgets the first wedding after the divorce," she insists. "I sat in the back of church practically laughing during the vows because the institution of marriage had become very 'unsacred' to me. At the reception, however, an old friend who had not heard about my situation asked me where my husband was. It was like I could not say the words, 'We are divorced.' I broke down completely and left the reception in tears."

You can anticipate these new situations with your friend, either by warning what might happen or by being present with your friend when—or after—they do.

If you know, for example, that your friend will be going to a high school or college reunion where the divorce is bound to come up, you can offer to accompany your friend, or meet afterwards, or at least "role play" how your friend will deal with the inevitable questions: "Yes, we've been happily divorced for two years" or "No, I never see my former spouse anymore."

For those divorced persons who have to keep in touch on a regular basis with their former spouses—usually because of children or finances—the rate of occurrence of setbacks can be even greater.

One man remembers feeling very strange after hanging up with his former wife after discussing finances. "I sat and listened to her talk to me about taking names off of credit cards and transferring money as though I was a new client in her office. When I hung up, all I could think about was that I had been married five years to a person I didn't ever know. I felt really weird for the rest of the night."

It is this "really weird" feeling that friends and family must be prepared to deal with. Setbacks come after the "numbness" caused by the acceptance of the reality of the divorce has set in, usually several months to a year after the final separation and divorce. Your divorced friend might even have begun to believe that he or she could see the light at the end of the tunnel, and then Boom! Bam!

□□□

The knowledge that, "It's gonna happen, ain't nothing you can do to prevent it" will be invaluable to both your friend and to you. It's also helpful to know that, while setbacks will continue to occur, they will finally begin to be fewer and fewer, and your friend's "comeback rate" will begin to get faster and faster. Your friend will still "freak out" or appear to "lose it," but eventually even that reaction will lessen.

The woman above who called her counselor after hearing of her former husband's engagement to another woman did go back to counseling, but only, it turned out, for two sessions. "I was surprised but relieved to find that I just needed a jump start after my battery went temporarily dead," she says. "I didn't need a whole new battery."

Strangely enough, setbacks can be sheep in wolves clothing. For as terrible as his or her reaction may be, your friend will discover that he or she feels even stronger following each set-back—especially if your are there to help him or her through it.

"Just think," you can say, "you made it through this before. I'm sure you can do it again. In fact, the last time was worse than this, and the next time it will be just a little easier."

The Little Engine did not get up the hill the first time. He went up once, fell back, got advice from the other engines, tried again, failed, regrouped and eventually made it. So will your friend.

Points to Remember

1. Your friend or relative can anticipate many setbacks while working through his or her divorce.

2. These setbacks are real, not imagined.

3. Usually, it's new situations that cause the greatest shocks.

4. "It's gonna happen, ain't nothin' you can do to prevent it" is the best attitude, but you can anticipate when the setbacks might occur and be there when they do.

5. The results and your friend's reactions to these setbacks will lessen over time, and the comeback rate will be quicker. They will eventually make your friend stronger.

RULE 9

RECLAIM THE GOOD

*T*he photograph my friend and I were looking at was of a very happy day, a day many years prior to my divorce. The faces in the picture were all smiling, and my former spouse had his arm around me. "That was a great day," my friend commented.

I remember fighting the urge to say something sarcastic like, "If I had only known then what I know now" or "Must not have been that great with the way things turned out." These types of comments had passed my lips before.

But as my friend continued reminiscing about the "great day," I felt a smile cross my lips.

She was right. It had been a great day. It suddenly occurred to me that even though I had been trying desperately to throw everything away that reminded me of my failed marriage, I should not disown a time that had at some points been "great."

"Yes, it was a great time," I admitted.

□□□

What my friend allowed me to do was to reclaim a good and happy part of my life, one that I thought I had to jettison with all the bad parts of my marriage.

As time goes on, your divorced friend or relative may have a hard time sorting through the memories of his or her failed marriage, deciphering which are "keepers" and what is excess baggage. You can be helpful to your friend when it comes time to deciding the good things to hold on to and the bad things to let go of. This clarity of distinguishing good from bad, healthy from unhealthy, helpful from harmful will help your friend begin to close some doors and leave others open.

□□□

You hope that, after a time, your friend will finally work through much of his or her denial and anger and grief and come to a certain degree of acceptance of the situation. Then it will be time to help him or her sort through the past and begin to understand the need to balance the pain and frustration with the memory of what was nice and pleasant and happy and even loving about the marriage that has ended.

Here is an analogy that may help—one my mother used with me to help me understand this point. Consider the purpose of high school yearbooks. They are supposed to provide happy memories of four important years in a person's life. The snapshots are of young people shooting basketballs, laughing in the cafeteria, studying in class; of teachers smiling and encouraging students. An occasional picture might remind you of the tears of an almost-victory or a sad moment at commencement, but for the most part, yearbooks attempt to capture the good times and very delicately gloss over the not-so-happy times.

I don't remember my yearbooks documenting the gigantic zit I developed the night before my senior prom or the time my best friend and I did not talk for days over some trivial matter. They don't mention the tension felt between the different cliques of kids in our school. There is no record of the big fat "F" I received on a math test or the personality struggle between my lockermate and the Biology teacher.

I know these things happened, but they weren't worth remembering or hanging on to, and the yearbook staff—wise beyond their years (or perhaps just well advised by the teacher moderator)—did not deem them worthy of inclusion.

You must become a yearbook editor for your friend's marriage.

□□□

Consider the time that your friend and his or her former spouse spent together in a marriage that ended so badly. Whether their marriage lasted years, months or even weeks, there must have been some good days. Certainly no couple ever walked down the wedding aisle hoping that their marriage would be filled with fights, tears, deceit and unhappiness. They wed because they believed that they could make a good life together.

"The hardest thing for me to accept in the divorce," one man admits, "was that it seemed to deny that we had once been happy. I know we had, because I can remember the good times. Our honeymoon—weren't we happy then? The day our first child was born—could we have been more in love?"

Yet marriages do end in divorce, as that of this man—and that of your friend—did. And they ended because the bad things outweighed the good. No survivor of a divorce—whether the divorce ended on civil terms or not, whether it was wanted by both parties or one, whether it was initiated by either party or both—wants to continue to relive the bad times.

Part of your job as a friend or relative is to give the divorced person permission to let go of those painful memories. Some people, often subconsciously, have a hard time letting go. They hold on to the worst parts of their marriage like a drowning person to a piece of wood. Perhaps it is a matter of fearing that if they stop feeling badly, they won't feel at all. Or maybe they are punishing themselves for their own contributions to the divorce by continuing to dwell on what went wrong. Whatever the reasons, holding tightly to these negative thoughts only prevents your friend from moving forward.

Some divorced people, for example, keep a "negative calendar" of events from the marriage. "It was three years ago today that I found out about her affair," they will say, or "I will never forget the time he hit me."

Those with regular contact with their former spouse often use the encounters as one more opportunity to rip off the scabs from their wounds. They fight about money, or visitation rights, or the children's education or health, but what they are really doing is trying to "hold on" to their former spouse—even in a totally negative way.

Other divorced people struggle with the issue of former in-laws and former friends. The death of a marriage also often means the end of many other relationships, but some divorced people are not willing to let them go. They either attempt to keep dead relationships alive or continually resent the fact that others choose not to keep in touch with them.

It is in situations like these that you should step in to remind your friend that he or she does have the power to either let go of these bad feelings or allow them to continue to gnaw at his or her insides. Your friend needs to understand that people often control the very emotions they believe are controlling them, that they are ultimately in charge of their own reactions to all that was bad in their marriages.

□□□

On the other hand, your friend might also need you to assure him or her that it is okay to retain some good memories from the failed marriage. Your friend may even feel guilty about having good feelings about the marriage. Perhaps he or she thinks that any positive emotions mean not really accepting the divorce or leaving the marriage behind. Maybe your friend is concerned that he or she secretly wants the former spouse back. Or possibly your friend is under the impression that admitting any good in the marriage is a betrayal of the support you have given.

One brother of a divorced woman told this story: "Everyone in the family was so supportive of my sister when the divorce first occurred. We all agreed that her former husband was a louse and had treated her wrong. Later, after she had gotten over her grief and anger, she began to remember some of the good things he had done, but she felt that she couldn't mention these to us. In fact, we wanted to be able to remember them, too, but we felt we'd be letting her down if we did!"

What you and your friend need to do is to make a "yearbook" of the marriage—one with the good things in and the bad things out. Then this "yearbook" can be symbolically put away—not to be browsed over every day, but always available when your friend needs it.

□□□

A different kind of terminology related to this dilemma of holding on/letting go is called "reconciliation versus resolution." This usually refers to those dealing with the grief over the death of a loved one, but it can also apply to the death of a marriage.

The term resolution suggests that a problem or a feeling will ultimately reach an end. Reconciliation means that the person will somehow come to a point of acceptance of a situation.

Your divorced friend wants resolution. All that can be attained is reconciliation. There will never be a time when your friend will feel that "the marriage never happened" or "my divorce is finally over." The best that can be hoped for is that your friend ultimately "comes to terms" with the loss of the marriage and moves on to a new life as a divorced person.

To accomplish this reconciliation, your friend will have to do two things: let go of all the bad things he or she has experienced and hold on to all the good things. Your job is to help your friend do both.

□□□

I must give credit to my mother again, who, with the grace of God, was able to make me see that I did have power over my own life and that I could make it either painful or joyful.

During my greatest stage of bitterness over my divorce, she told me a story of a woman in her bridge group who had been divorced many years before. The woman spoke to my mother of her divorce only once. She said, "I was married many years ago to a good person. Unfortunately, the marriage did not work out. I have a very happy life now."

When Mom told me that story, I suddenly realized how I wanted to think and speak about my own divorce. I wanted to be free of my anger and pain, but I did not want to deny my marriage or forget the good parts of my life then.

It took me many years to get to that place, but that is where I now am. I got here primarily because of the help of my family and friends. Your friend will too.

Points to Remember

1. You will have to help your friend or relative hold on to the good memories and let go of the bad memories from his or her marriage.

2. You need to become a "yearbook" editor for your friend's marriage.

3. There may be many reasons why your friend cannot let go of the negative parts of his or her marriage. You may need to give him or her permission to do so.

4. The best that your friend can hope for is to become reconciled to the divorce, rather than expecting his or her feelings to be resolved.

5. Your friend will finally get to the place he or she needs to be...with your help.

RULE 10

I was having a serious crisis regarding my choice of clothes for the evening. I was sweating. I panicked. My sister called. Then my mother called. Then I called both of them. I dreaded the next five hours.

I was a thirty-one-year-old adult. A mother. A high school English teacher. And a woman about to experience her "first date" for only the second time in her entire life.

I found myself suddenly angry at my former husband for putting me in this situation, even though I knew that the present was better than the past.

□□□

The most potentially deceiving period for helping your friend or relative through a divorce comes last. It is the time when most friends and relatives believe that their work of support is over and no longer needed. It is the longest period of time, for it will last the rest of both of your lives. It is the long haul.

Once your friend seems to be over the initial "grieving" stage of the divorce, once the "setbacks" have become few and far between, you might find yourself pleased and relieved that the two of you have reached the finish line. You would be incorrect.

The truth is that your friend will be divorced for the rest of his or her life—even if he or she happily remarries. The traumas, the issues, the changes brought about by divorce are too deep and too important to ever disappear completely—no matter how much both you and your friend would like them to.

If you are going to truly help your friend through a divorce, you've got to stay for the long haul.

When my sister and my mother held my hand through my first post-divorce date, I'm sure they'd rather have been doing almost anything else. But they had made a commitment to me to see me through to the end. And they have. They have seen me through the divorce and raising my son as a single mom and my first date and my marriage to another. And they are not through yet! Remarried or not, I will always be divorced, and I will always need their presence and support in dealing with that fact.

□□□

Most storms do permanent damage. So do most divorces. First comes the great winds of grief and anger and other emotions. Then there are the aftershocks of many setbacks. Finally, there is a false calm. You begin to see great hope in your friend's eyes. Real rebuilding begins to take place.

Yet I guarantee you that your friend is still on shaky ground. That storm has left damage that is not apparent on the surface but can affect any attempt to build a new life. Your support is as necessary now as it was on the day your friend first told you about the divorce.

Remember that your friend has experienced one of the greatest examples of loss and betrayal of which humans are capable— the breakup of a marriage. This experience will color everything else he or she attempts to do and every relationship he or she attempts to have. It will affect your friend's child-rearing, family relationships, friendships, work life, spirituality and even future marriage.

Not that all the changes your divorced friend has gone through are bad. In fact, especially if you have done your job well as family or friend, your friend could be a stronger, better person because of—not despite—the divorce. It's just that you and your friend both need to realize that recovery from a divorce is a lifelong task.

□□□

One obvious area of concern for the long haul is trust. No matter who was "responsible" or "at fault" for the divorce, it is certain that trust was destroyed. Having experienced first-hand the fragility of trust, your friend will be naturally cautious about giving it again quickly or freely.

This fear of trust can show itself in many ways. In the raising of children, for example, divorced people may send (sometimes very unintentionally) messages to their children that "people (or especially people of the opposite sex) are not to be trusted." Divorced parents can also often undermine their children's development of trust by constantly criticizing the other parent or by second guessing or putting down the other parent's lifestyle or parenting decisions.

Sometimes it is your role as a friend or relative to remind the divorced person that his or her words or attitudes will have a profound affect on the children.

This same problem with trust can carry over into every aspect of your divorced friend's life. The loss of trust in the marriage may become a loss of trust in the workplace, with other family members, even with other friends—like you! One of your responsibilities as the friend of a divorced person is to be a model of trust-worthiness and fidelity, to prove to your friend that trust between two people is possible and is, in fact, the norm.

□□□

Another area for the long haul can be finances and living conditions. Many divorced people—especially women—experience a severe drop in income and living conditions after a divorce. The number of single-parent families that end up poor and on welfare is a national disgrace.

You may be called upon to help out in a variety of ways. Depending on your own circumstances, you may need to give the divorced person some extra money at holidays or for their children. Or you may get involved in finding employment for your friend or helping to provide child care while your friend works. In a few cases, especially if the divorced person is a family member, you may even end up living together!

If you have a relationship with both divorced spouses, you may even serve a mediator function, convincing one partner to share resources more equitably with the other.

No, you didn't ask for any of this. It may not even be the appropriate role for you. But, someone has got to help the divorced person through the shoals of finances and living conditions, and it may just turn out to be you.

□□□

Another huge area that you may be called upon to help your friend with is the question of dating and even remarriage. Here is where you will need the wisdom of Solomon, the patience of Job, the courage of Ruth...and the humor of Lily Tomlin.

One woman remembers what she thought about dating after she and her husband separated. "I truly believed that the whole thing was kind of like getting bucked off a horse," she says. "My dad always told me to get right back on. I thought that in order to fix the problem or make the pain go away I needed to get right back out there and start dating again. What a mistake!"

This woman was not alone. Many divorced persons jump into dating at a time when dating may be the last thing they need to be doing, and their friends egg them on. Many friends and relatives spend a great deal of time attempting to set up their divorced friends for dates, either because they think it's a good idea or because they don't think at all.

Another woman remembers that everyone in her workplace had someone in mind for her. "A day would not pass without someone coming up with the 'perfect guy,'" she remembers. "One man was very angry when I told him I wasn't interested. He said, 'If you're not married or dating anyone else, why won't you just go out for dinner?' He couldn't understand that I was just not ready to date."

You should remind you friend that newly divorced people are very vulnerable and therefore more likely to get romantically involved for the wrong reasons. Your friend also should understand that a person can be "not dating" and yet not lonely.

□□□

No alarm clock will go off signaling the right time for your friend to start dating. He or she will need to decide that for himself or herself. Your job as a friend, however, is to raise the right questions.

One divorced man remembers dating different women every weekend. Although he was not getting involved with many of them, he wishes in retrospect that a friend would have pulled him aside and asked him what he was doing. "From all appearances, I seemed fine," he explains. "Probably even great. But I think I was trying to fill a void in my life that resulted when my wife left me. I know now that I could have filled that void with other things."

Another woman remembers declaring to her family that she would never date again. "So many people around me were so affected by my divorce that I knew that I never wanted to get divorced again," she says. "The only way I could insure that would be if I never married again, so why date? I knew I wasn't ready at that time, but I also knew I was choosing not to date for the wrong reason."

If this woman's family and friends had assured her that they were with her no matter what her decisions and even if she should fail again at marriage, she would have been able to make her dating decision based on her own need and not on her perception of other's needs.

Finally, your friend may someday announce plans to marry a new spouse. Your friendship will be once more called upon—first as a touchstone upon which to measure the wisdom of the decision, and then as a rock on which to support the decision. There are no absolutes. Some divorced people probably should never remarry. Others might do so successfully right after their divorce is final. Most should wait a considerable length of time to be sure that they have truly recovered from their previous marriage and are not "rebounding" into another.

Through all this, you will be expected to be there for your friend. It is indeed a long haul.

□□□

There is one other change that will take place over the long haul. Your relationship with your friend will also change.

Remember that divorce touches almost every aspect of your friend's life—from living conditions to parenting situation to social life. It only makes sense that the divorce will affect how your and your friend relate to each other.

One woman remembers: "Nothing is the same now. That's not such a bad deal. I am sad for the old friends that are not such great friends anymore. I am happy for the people to whom I've become closer because of divorce. Little did I know that the day I became single again would change everything, but more than anything I changed. I had to in order to move forward."

If you can understand that your divorced friend needs to change to survive and grow, then you may well find that the divorce itself has made your relationship that much more rewarding and fulfilling, even if different than it was. My sister and mother made it through that "second first date" with me that night, and it brought the three of us that much closer together, even though our relationship was just a little bit different from then on.

I never had to call them before a date again. I got a little more confident that night. I grew a little more. But I always knew that they would be there when I needed them. They were with me for the long haul.

Points to Remember

1. Your divorced friend or relative needs you for the long haul.

2. Your friend's divorce will affect his or her child-rearing, family relationships, friendships, work life, spirituality and even future marriage.

3. One of your jobs as a friend is to model trustworthiness and fidelity by your words and actions.

4. You may be called upon to help with your friend's finances, living conditions, dating and remarriage. You may not have asked for the responsibility, but what are friends for?

5. Among the multitude of things that will change with your friend's divorce is the two of your relationship.

POINTS TO REMEMBER

☐ Emotions are neither right nor wrong, they just are.

☐ There will be a variety of emotions caused by the divorce of a friend or relative.

☐ It is important for you to get in touch with your emotions about the divorce, both for your own peace of mind and so you can be more helpful to your friend.

☐ It is not necessary that you share all of your feelings immediately with your friend. You will know when the time has come to do so, and then be sure to do so gently.

☐ Your friend may not be able to deal with his or her emotions about the divorce as quickly as you do. Don't drift away or become frustrated when he or she takes time.

☐ Your friend needs you to keep reaching out. He or she will respond when ready.

☐ It is your job to initiate the contacts. It is too much to expect your friend to do it. You have to take the risk of being rejected.

☐ Sometimes, especially in the beginning, all your friend needs is a willing listener and a warm hug. You don't have to have all the answers.

☐ Your offers of help must be as specific as possible. Take "no" for an answer, but don't hesitate to repeat the offer.

☐ Your reaching out must continue for a long time, even years.

☐ Being a friend to a divorced person is not easy.

- [ ] Your presence is the most important gift you can give to your friend.

- [ ] Your friend may not always be receptive to you. Don't use that as an excuse to stay away.

- [ ] You will make lots of mistakes while trying to support your friend or relative through a divorce. Each divorce is unique, don't expect to have all the answers.

- [ ] All this might make your relationship stronger, better, deeper.

- [ ] Your friend will most likely experience a loss of self-esteem after the divorce. Remind your friend that he or she is still loved and lovable.

- [ ] Your friend or relative needs to accept his or her new identity as a divorced person.

- [ ] Your job is not to protect your friend from this new identity but to encourage him or her to get on with life.

- [ ] Try to be of specific help to your friend in establishing his or her new identity. Pick up a phone. Check something out. Go with your friend on a first visit.

- [ ] You now have a divorced friend. Your identity has now changed also, no matter how slightly. Accept it and work within it.

- [ ] Divorce is tragedy, but it can also at times be comedy.

- [ ] Your friend needs you to help keep humor alive. Look for the humor in the situation.

- [ ] You are the judge of what and when humor is appropriate. You will make mistakes, but you need to risk them.

- [ ] Monitor your humor around the children. Remember that they won't always understand it.

- [ ] Don't let your friend's humor become self-deprecating or mean-spirited.

- [ ] The year is full of holidays, anniversaries and special dates relating to the marriage and divorce that will affect your friend or relative.

- [ ] You need to mark your own holiday and anniversary calendar to remind yourself of your friend's special dates, especially during the first year following the divorce.

- [ ] You do not necessarily need to mention the divorce when you contact your friend on special dates, but you also should be prepared for his or her reaction.

- [ ] Although your presence will ease your friend's pain, it cannot erase the pain.

- [ ] The first year following the divorce will end eventually and things will get easier, but you will still need to be sensitive to your friend's feelings and situation.

- [ ] Change is difficult for all of us because of our fear of the unknown.

- [ ] Your divorced friend or relative is facing the future without the partner he or she planned for and after trust has been broken at least once.

- ☐ Your friend needs you to keep insisting that he or she keep moving forward, even if your advice is sometimes unwelcome.

- ☐ Sometimes the best help you can give to your friend is to suggest professional help.

- ☐ You also need to keep moving forward and not allow your own fears and uncertainties to get you stuck.

- ☐ Your friend or relative can anticipate many setbacks while working through his or her divorce.

- ☐ These setbacks are real, not imagined.

- ☐ Usually, it's new situations that cause the greatest shocks.

- ☐ "It's gonna happen, ain't nothin' you can do to prevent it" is the best attitude, but you can anticipate when the setbacks might occur and be there when they do.

- ☐ The results and your friend's reactions to these setbacks will lessen over time, and the comeback rate will be quicker. They will eventually make your friend stronger.

- ☐ You will have to help your friend or relative hold on to the good memories and let go of the bad memories from his or her marriage.

- ☐ You need to become a "yearbook" editor for your friend's marriage.

- ☐ There may be many reasons why your friend cannot let go of the negative parts of his or her marriage. You may need to give him or her permission to do so.

☐ The best that your friend can hope for is to become reconciled to the divorce, rather than expecting his or her feelings to be resolved.

☐ Your friend will finally get to the place he or she needs to be...with your help.

☐ Your divorced friend or relative needs you for the long haul.

☐ Your friend's divorce will affect his or her child-rearing, family relationships, friendships, work life, spirituality and even future marriage.

☐ One of your jobs as a friend is to model trustworthiness and fidelity by your words and actions.

☐ You may be called upon to help with your friend's finances, living conditions, dating and remarriage. You may not have asked for the responsibility, but what are friends for?

☐ Among the multitude of things that will change with your friend's divorce is the two of your relationship.

RESOURCES TO RECOMMEND TO YOUR FRIEND

KIDS/TEENS ARE NONDIVORCEABLE by Sara Bonkowski. These two companion volumes are specifically written for parents trying to help their children deal with the parents' divorce. *Kids Are Nondivorceable* for children 6-11 years old (128 pages, $7.95); *Teens Are Nondivorceable* for children 12-18 years old (160 pages, $7.95).

LIVES UPSIDE DOWN: SURVIVING DIVORCE by James Flosi. Uses actual stories of divorcing people and their children to illustrate the four "stages" that most divorces go through (96 pages, $5.95).

ANNULMENT: A STEP BY GUIDE FOR DIVORCED CATHOLICS by Ronald T. Smith. This helpful, up-to-date guide provides practical information about each of the steps involved in the annulment process, along with helpful insights into healing and moving forward with one's personal and spiritual life (112 pages, $8.95).

DIVORCE AND BEYOND by James Greteman and Leon Haverkamp. This support-group program for newly divorced persons focuses on the "mourning period" of the divorce process and concentrates mainly in the divorced persons themselves, rather than on their role as parents. Participant's Book (132 pages, $4.95); Facilitator's Manual (80 pages, $4.95).

TO TRUST AGAIN by William Urbine. A complete, self-contained program for marriage preparation for couples in which one or both parties have been involved in a previous marriage which ended through death or divorce. Couple's Workbook (48 pages, $4.95); Leader's Guide (48 pages, $9.95); Remarriage Inventory (32 pages, $4.95).

MEDITATIONS (WITH SCRIPTURE) FOR BUSY MOMS by Patricia Robertson. Insightful, down-to-earth reflections for each day of the year paired with surprising and illuminating quotes from the Bible (368 pages, $8.95).

MEDITATIONS (WITH SCRIPTURE) FOR BUSY DADS by Patrick T. Reardon. A companion to the Moms book just for Dads (368 pages, $8.95).